MW01611769

I WONDER AS
I WANDER

The 12 Days of Christmas
with MADELEINE L'ENGLE

Anamchara Books
Vestal, New York 13850
www.AnamcharaBooks.com

Paperback ISBN: 978-1-62524-483-3
Ebook ISBN: 978-1-62524-486-4

Illustrations by Iatsun (Dreamstime)
or from the public domain.

Design by Micaela Grace.

I WONDER AS
I WANDER

The 12 Days of Christmas
with MADELEINE L'ENGLE

BRUCE G. EPPERLY

CONTENTS

1. **A Swiftly Moving Season**   9

2. **A Story-Shaping Spirituality**   17

3. **Adventures in Incarnation**   23

4. **The Heartbeat of Christmas**   29

THE 12 DAYS OF CHRISTMAS
Days of Awe and Wonder

5. **Prelude: Christmas Eve**
      December 24   35

6. **The First Day of Christmas**
      December 25   43

7. **The Second Day of Christmas**
      December 26—*The Feast of St. Stephen*   51

8. **The Third Day of Christmas**
   December 27   **57**

9. **The Fourth Day of Christmas**
   December 28   **63**

10. **The Fifth Day of Christmas**
    December 29   **69**

11. **The Sixth Day of Christmas**
    December 30   **75**

12. **The Seventh Day of Christmas**
    December 31   **81**

13. **The Eighth Day of Christmas**
    January 1   **87**

14. **The Ninth Day of Christmas**
    January 2   **93**

15. **The Tenth Day of Christmas**
    January 3   **99**

16. **The Eleventh Day of Christmas**
   January 4   **105**

17. **The Twelfth Day of Christmas**
   January 5   **112**

18. **Postlude: Wandering Forward**
   January 6—*The Feast of Epiphany*   **119**

19. **Books to Live By**
   Wandering with Madeleine L'Engle   **127**

.1.
A SWIFTLY MOVING SEASON

I wonder as I wander out under the sky.

(John Jacob Niles)

The sense of wonder is a prayer.

(Madeleine L'Engle, *Genesis Trilogy*)

Christmas is a swiftly moving season with few clear boundaries. The day after we've packed up our Halloween costumes, Hallmark Channel begins nearly two months of twenty-four-seven presentations of Christmas movies. Shortly thereafter, we are inundated by ads inviting us to shop early to get the best bargains. The holiday rush is in full swing by Thanksgiving with Black Friday and Cyber Monday sales abounding, and people jostling one another to be first to purchase the latest "must-have" Christmas presents. Radio stations begin playing Christmas songs on Thanksgiving Day.

In the fifty-five days from All Saints' Day to Christmas Day, we prepare for Christ's coming through on-line shopping, bargain hunting, photos with Santa, songs and carols, baking, drinking, and reveling. Despite wars and rumors of war, poverty, addiction, and homelessness, Christmas magic is in the air! But often in the magic we miss the sacredness of the season, the holy time and space of pregnancy, birth, and revelation.

The Challenge of Christmas

As a pastor, I find celebrating the Christmas season challenging. The Cape Cod congregation I pastor holds a cantata and Christmas pageant on the third and fourth Sundays of Advent, respectively, and we sing carols on the first Sunday of December during our village's annual Christmas stroll.

Meanwhile, like most Americans, I wander the aisles and surf the Web, looking for the right gifts for each person on my list. I hum Christmas carols in the wake of Thanksgiving dinner and visit Santa Claus with my grandchildren. I have to remind myself that the Christmas season begins on December 25 and not on an arbitrary date that was determined by advertising agencies, big-box and on-line stores, and movie releases. I struggle with preserving the Advent tradition of waiting, living in the tension between now and not-yet, the Christ that comes to a world still looking for peace on Earth, goodwill to all.

The Season of Incarnation has been rendered superficial by movies, kitschy songs, and consumerism. The Twelve Days of Christmas have become a prelude to Christmas Day, rather than a time of spiritual reflection between December 25 and January 5. By Boxing Day, December 26, most of us are worn out and ready to move on to secular time once more. The mystery and messiness of what Madeleine L'Engle describes as the "irrational season" is drowned out by the banality of "Jingle Bell Rock" and "Santa Baby"!

How can we recover the meaning of this season? I think it will only happen with intention and commitment to quiet moments in the midst of the frantic busyness of shopping, baking, wrapping, and decorating. Whether we are pastors, active church members, or spiritual seekers of any ilk, we need to pause now and then during the Christmas season and let the wonder of the Incarnation soak in. Images and questions will emerge if we allow ourselves to move more gently through the twelve days of the Christmas season. In moments of stillness, we can begin again to pay attention to the amazing news of God's Word and Wisdom, the Energy of Love (the same Love that brought billions of stars out of the darkness) being birthed in the chaos on a small, blue-green planet barely noticeable in the immensity of the Milky Way.

On Christmas night, after packages are unwrapped and leftovers placed in the refrigerator, we need to pause awhile and take a deep spiritual breath, as the parents of bride and groom often do following the departure of the last guests at the wedding reception, to give thanks, awaken to the Holy Here and Now, and ponder the amazing and unexpected synergy of Divine and human love. This quiet, tired moment is an opportunity to remember that once the packages are unwrapped, dishes washed, trash taken out, and decorations taken down, the journey of Christmas, like the journey of marriage, is only just beginning. The ceremonies of marriage and Christmas are merely the first steps of holy adventures that take us to unknown lands.

We need at least twelve days to let the real magic of Christmas soak in—the Infinite God, Divine Word and Wisdom, taking flesh in the messiness of a stable, among strangers and outsiders, in an occupied land. We need to awaken to the "impossible possibility" that God is also being birthed in the chaos of our world, amid the threat of nuclear war, the reckless bloviations of political leaders and the realities of addiction, poverty, racism, privilege, and environmental degradation. We need time to wonder, to imagine big possibilities and ask important questions as we wander outside our typical comfort zones, exploring new ways to celebrate the season as we go beyond the traditions and theologies of our own congregations and cultures.

The Story Behind This Book

During the 2016 Advent and Christmas seasons, I began a spiritual practice as a way of celebrating the twelve days of Christmas in a new and creative way. In the weeks prior to Christmas, I immersed myself in the works of African American theologian and mystic, Howard Thurman, and selected a number of inspirational passages which, along with my Scripture study, would serve as the centerpiece of my daily Christmas devotions and the writing of *The Work of Christmas: The Twelve Days of Christmas with Howard Thurman.* A year later, I chose to reflect on the writings of author Madeleine L'Engle, letting her spiritual and autobiographical reflections and young adult books shape my Christmas devotions. Each day, I read a passage from L'Engle's writing along with scriptural accounts of Jesus' conception and birth, and then I meditated on these passages as I took my morning walk in the frigid winter air on Craigville and Covell's beaches on Cape Cod and through the quaint Craigville neighborhood. When I returned home, I spent a few minutes writing down any insights that emerged on my pilgrimages through my Cape Cod neighborhood. I also listened to Christmas carols and read about the saints' days of the Christmas season, and integrated these into my prayer life and personal reflections. These inspirations gave birth to *I Wonder as I Wander.*

If Rabbi Abraham Joshua Heschel is correct in his belief that radical amazement is at the heart of religious experience, then wondering can be a spiritual discipline. Moreover, as Jimmy Buffet says, changes in latitude may lead to changes in attitude. Physical movement often liberates spiritual and intellectual insights. In joining wondering and wandering, I let the questions and images flow as I opened to God's wisdom and creativity.

Christmas is amazing—and radical. It challenges wanderers to let their imaginations run wild. Christmas is an irrational, impossible, paradoxical season—the infinite in the finite, God's light in the gloom of our world, the wholeness of the universe concentrated in a little baby, the God of the Big Bang and galaxies appearing in a homeless, working class, and soon-to-be-refugee family.

My hope is that you will both wonder and wander during the Christmas Season, with a star orienting your spiritual GPS. In the twelve days of Christmas, bookended by Christmas Eve and the Feast of Epiphany, may you be sensitive to the awe and wonder of the Incarnation. As you experience the many births of Christ in your life and in our world, I pray that you will embody, in the gloom of our time, the wisdom of J.R.R. Tolkien, who wrote that "not all who wander are lost."

.2.

A STORY-SHAPING FAITH

Stories, no matter how simple,
can be vehicles of truth;
can be, in fact, icons.
Jesus taught almost entirely
by telling stories, simple stories dealing
with the stuff of his day.
Stories are able to help us be more
whole, to be Named.

(Madeleine L'Engle, *Walking on Water*)

Madeleine L'Engle once noted that her stories shaped her faith as much as her faith shaped her stories. Christmas is the season of stories: tales of Magi following a star, angelic visitations, foreign visitors, and the birth of a child a humble stable.

Christmas defies any quest for factual verification, whether from literalist preachers or deconstructionist Bible scholars. While there is some benefit in seeking the "facts" of Christmas, the truth of Christmas goes beyond the unimaginative explanations of fundamentalist and deconstructionist alike. The stories of Christmas invite us to go beyond the five senses and one-dimensional facts, to peer into the heart of God, to discern the Divine in ordinary events, and recognize that reality is always more than meets the eye.

Like fairy tales and legends, Christmas points to a magic reality—a thin place—where miracles happen and healings occur. Literalistic scholarship and preaching tethers us to too closely to the earth, while the reality of Christmas turns our imagination's gaze toward a wondrous star, a child chockfull of divinity, and shepherds and Magi who behold God incarnate in a newborn child. Christmas is the "impossible possibility" that transforms our lives and inspires art, literature, theology, and everyday acts of kindness. Christmas reminds us that we are all storytellers, if we allow ourselves to be, artistically creating new Christmas visions to be embodied in our world in partnership with the Artist of Creation.

In one of my favorite films, *Chariots of Fire,* Olympic runner and later missionary to China Eric Liddell exclaims, "I believe God made me for a purpose. God made me fast, and when I run, I feel God's pleasure." Something similar could be said for Madeleine L'Engle: her writing was an expression of Divine pleasure. She confessed that writing was God's gift to her, and she saw her writing as a pathway to wholeness. Although some tried to pin her down—and thus marginalize her—as a Christian children's and young adults' writer, she rebelled against such descriptions. While rooted in the Christ-Story, L'Engle saw her work as global in spirit.

Like the Logos theologians of the early centuries of Christianity, L'Engle believed that wherever truth is found, God is its source, even if truth ranges far beyond the boundaries of so-called "orthodox" Christianity or Christian faith itself. In the spirit of C. S. Lewis, J.R.R. Tolkien, Charles Williams, and George Macdonald, her stories are rooted on earth but ascend to the heavens, and in the process, they illuminate everyday life with God's grandeur.

She knew that imaginative writing, like the best of theological reflection, is open to the contributions of science, literature, poetry, fairy tales, and the insights and wisdom of sages from every religious tradition. She pondered the Big Bang, quantum physics, psychology, and theology. Beneath a simple story, perhaps a teenage quest for meaning and the experience of first love, was hidden the treasure of Divine revelation.

In the spirit of the Celtic Christianity and its pagan precursors, L'Engle believed that any place could be a "thin place," translucent to the living God. With only a stone for a pillow, you may find yourself dreaming of a ladder of angels, as Jacob did, and awaken exclaiming, "God was in this place and I did not know it!" In your closet, you may find a mysterious portal to Narnia. Sitting on a stone in a Connecticut woodland, you may tesseract into new dimensions of time and space.

A wise saying proclaims, *solvitur ambulando*—it will be solved in the walking. Wanderers and adventurers discover wonders that elude those who are content to live within the boundaries of the known world. Madeleine L'Engle found inspirations in her country walks and beside a stream near her family's home in Goshen, Connecticut.

I find my inspiration walking along Cape Cod beaches. My morning perambulations on the Craigville and Covell's beaches near my home in Centerville, Massachusetts, awaken me to the *plus ultra*, the "something more," that inspires and transforms an ordinary day into an icon of Divine love. In fact, as I strolled on Craigville Beach and through the historic Craigville neighborhood near my home, the inspiration for this book and its predecessor emerged. "Out of nowhere," I felt a lure to deepen my Christian faith by living with the Christmas stories.

In a similar fashion, as L'Engle walked the woods of rural Connecticut, she discovered that "it will be solved in the writing," as well as in walking. In reflective hours dedicated to research and writing, she found meaning, direction, and healing. In those quiet hours, L'Engle experienced the Incarnation as a living reality, found in the complicated dance of writing, marriage, parenting, and teaching.

Like all pilgrims, L'Engle was well aware of her limitations. She often quoted Augustine, "If you think you know it, it isn't God." She knew, with the fourth-century theologian, that authentic spiritual growth embraces rather than excludes doubt. Yet, like the Magi, she followed a star, seeking wisdom in everyday life and in contemplating the cosmic forces within which we live and move and have our being. She discovered that Christ is born everywhere, in cells as well as souls, for those with eyes to see and hearts to feel.

.3.
ADVENTURES
IN INCARNATION

The artist, who is a Christian,
like any other Christian,
is required to be in this world,
but not of it.
We are to be in this world as healers,
as listeners, and as servants.

(Madeleine L'Engle, *Walking on Water*)

Madeleine L'Engle was born to a family of both privilege and challenge. Her parents could afford to send her, sometimes to her sorrow and chagrin, to boarding schools, where she garnered a strong literary and intellectual foundation. Her father was a journalist, foreign correspondent, and literary critic, with many social and cultural connections among the elite of his time. He was also, however, plagued with poor health, due to contact with mustard gas while serving in Europe during World War II. He died when she was seventeen and away from home at boarding school. Perhaps her youthful grief is reflected in writing that recognizes the interplay of brevity and insecurity with the wonder and beauty of life. On a star-filled night, L'Engle discovered, with the troubled lower-class shepherds, the meaning of the angelic counsel, "Fear not, God is with you."

L'Engle admitted that although she was steeped in Anglican liturgy, she had very little formal religious training as a child. She believed that in many ways her lack of childhood catechetical education was a gift. She had little to unlearn later in life and could come to faith with fresh eyes, without the confines of biblical literalism or narrow-minded prejudice.

Young Madeleine L'Engle was a bit like a geode, whose inner beauty is often hidden by a nondescript or rough-hewn exterior. Like Charles Wallace of her Time Trilogy tales, she was often underestimated by her teachers, who seldom saw her as a budding intellectual or promising writer. She was criticized for "coloring outside the lines" when her responses to assignments were too imaginative or creative to fit into the academic boxes constructed by her teachers. Nevertheless, Madeleine was born to be a writer. She wrote her first story at age five and began journaling at age eight.

Youthful Madeleine began to find her voice and discover her vocation while studying at Smith College. Following graduation from college, she sought a career in the theatre. During her theatre years, she met and married a fellow actor, Hugh Franklin (1916–1986), best-known for his role as Dr. Charles Tyler in the long-running soap opera, *All My Children*.

In the early 1950s, Madeleine and Hugh left Manhattan to live in Goshen, Connecticut, where they ran a general store, and Madeleine served as the choir director of the local Congregational church. Although she published two books by her mid-thirties, she almost gave up writing at forty, believing that she needed to carry her weight in the family finances. Success came at last in 1962 with the award-winning *Wrinkle in Time*, finally published after twenty-six publishers' rejections.

Over the next four decades, L'Engle wrote more than thirty books, ranging from children's and young adult literature to poetry and theological and spiritual reflections. Nothing was off-limits to her creative mind, whether in science, literature, theology, or Scripture. She could find holiness in a teenage romance, the tale of a biblical patriarch or matriarch, a scientific experiment, the smile of a dolphin, or tesseracting from one dimension one another.

As a writer, L'Engle's quest for wholeness was inspired by her vision of the writing process as something that both gives glory to God and brings joy and insight to children, adolescents, and adults. Her depth as a writer emerged from the interplay of inspiration and intentionality, nurtured by a committed prayer life.

She began each day with prayer. At day's end, she concluded with prayer, inspired by the words of the Episcopalian *Book of Common Prayer*. The Jesus Prayer, "Lord have mercy upon me, a sinner," was her constant mental companion, running alongside her commitment to silent listening for Divine inspiration. She also had a regular practice of visualizing persons and situations in terms of wholeness and possibility.

L'Engle found that the spiritual journey for writers—and all spiritual pilgrims—comes down to the practice of kything, described in her Time Trilogy, the practice of empathetic communication that joins two people or a group with one another whether side by side or across the universe.

L'Engle's books promote this living spiritual connection in their readers. In experiences of imaginative empathy, awe, and wonder, and reflections on her own childhood and youth, she used her writing to connect with every season and facet of life. Her books continue to inspire young children, ambivalent teens, questioning laypeople, and experienced pastors to see divinity hidden in the wondrous and inspiring disarray of this Holy Here and Now.

.4.

THE HEARTBEAT
OF CHRISTMAS

God is over all things,
under all things,
outside all,
within, but not all,
without, but not
excluded,
above, but not
raised up,
below, but not depressed,
wholly above,
presiding,
wholly without, embracing,
wholly within, filling.

(Hildevert of Lavartan, eleventh-century mystic)

The incarnation of God, reflected in L'Engle's affirmation of Hildevert's poetic wisdom, proclaims that the Child born in a Bethlehem stable reveals God's wondrous love for Creation. The Infinite takes birth in the uncertainty, chaos, and tragic beauty of Creation among marginalized and dispossessed persons. Soon the baby's family would have to run for their lives, like millions in our world today, to escape political violence.

According to Madeleine L'Engle, the Incarnation proclaims, "Christ, the Second Person of the Trinity, the Maker of the universe or perhaps many universes, willingly and lovingly left all that power and came to this sin-filled planet to show us what we ought to be and could be" (*Bright Evening Star*, paraphrase). The Divine becomes human so that humanity can embrace its own holiness and divinity. The Christ Child comes to our world so that the Christ present in each and every child may take birth amid the challenges of our time and place.

The Incarnation is neither arbitrary or supernatural, but reflects God's ever-present, dynamic, and creative Wisdom. The world is chockfull with Divinity. Madeleine believed this as firmly as did the ancient theologian who stated, "God is the circle whose center is everywhere and whose circumference is nowhere." God is not an alien, outside thing but rather the heartbeat of Creation, the pulse giving life to stars and cells, and inspiring the mystic quest. As Gerard Manley Hopkins affirms, "the world is charged with God's grandeur." God's Spirit is bonded to our world, energizing and reconciling all things, experiencing our woe as well as our joy. Despite the suffering and destruction humankind wreaks upon the world, the planet is not exhausted or doomed, because, in Hopkins' words,

> *the Holy Ghost over the bent*
> *World broods with warm breast and with ah! bright wings.*

God's heart beats in Mary's womb and in every child born on this good Earth. God's new creation stirs hope for peace on Earth, goodwill to all. Without God's incarnate love, our world would be lost and hope in the future a phantasm.

Although the Incarnation is not a supernatural intrusion into a godless world, the wonder of the Christmas message transcends any explanation or doctrine within which we might confine it. Some try to fathom the Incarnation, believing that everything must make literal sense, and the coming of Jesus must be exactly as the Bible describes. Others try to debunk the Christmas stories as fictional. Yet the birth of Jesus, like the conception of every child, will always be an unfathomable mystery.

Ultimately, the Incarnation comes down to the affirmation that love is stronger than hate, life embraces death, and hope transcends fear. The Christ Child, who joins humanity and Divinity, time and eternity, and finite and infinite, reveals the love that brings the world into being and lures us toward wholeness in a world of tragedy and injustice.

The Incarnation is ultimately about God's love for mortal flesh and lively Creation. "We are, every one of us," L'Engle avers, "even at our most difficult, within the love of Jesus, who was born for us" (*Bright Morning Star*). While many Christmas see the heart of Christianity as the affirmation that "Christ died for us," L'Engle proclaims, "Christ was born for us." Wherever there is love, Jesus is our companion, even if we don't recognize his presence.

The Herods and Augustus Caesars of this world will be forgotten, empires will rise and empires will fall, but the heartbeat of the universe, lovingly beating in Bethlehem, will last forever. Do not be afraid, for God is with us!

THE 12 DAYS
OF CHRISTMAS

Days of Awe and Wonder

.5.

PRELUDE: CHRISTMAS EVE

(DECEMBER 24)

In the sixth month the angel Gabriel was sent by God to a town in Galilee called Nazareth, to a vir-
gin engaged to a man whose name was Joseph, of the house of David. The virgin's name was Mary. And he came to her and said, "Greetings, favored one! The Lord is with you." But she was

much perplexed by his words and pondered what sort of greeting this might be. The angel said to her, "Do not be afraid, Mary, for you have found favor with God. . . . And now, your relative Elizabeth in her old age has also conceived a son; and this is the sixth month for her who was said to be barren. For nothing will be impossible with God." Then Mary said, "Here am I, the servant of the Lord; let it be with me according to your word." Then the angel departed from her.

(Luke 1:26–30, 38–40)

Now the birth of Jesus the Messiah took place in this way. When his mother Mary had been engaged to Joseph, but before they lived together, she was found to be with child from the Holy Spirit. Her husband Joseph, being a righteous man and unwilling to expose her to public disgrace, planned to dismiss her quietly. But just when he had resolved to do this, an angel of the Lord appeared to him in a dream and said, "Joseph, son of David, do not be afraid to take Mary as your wife, for the child conceived in her is from the Holy Spirit."

(Matthew 1:18–20)

The only God who seems
to be worth believing
is impossible for mortal man
to understand,
and therefore teaches us
through the impossible.

(Madeleine L'Engle, *The Irrational Season*)

There is also a legend that Mary
was not the first young woman to
whom the angel came.
But she was the first one to say yes.

(Madeleine L'Engle, *The Genesis Trilogy*)

In the great "once upon a time" of Jesus' conception and birth, a young girl encountered an angel who was asking the impossible from someone so young and inexperienced. In response, she did something equally impossible: she said "yes" to the Great Mystery, to the Infinite Godhead taking birth in her finite, mortal flesh. She had no pious words in response and did not fully comprehend what was happening to her, and yet she willingly shared in the miracle, the greatest miracle of all—the birth of a Child, the Divine, the Love that brought forth the universe, that spun galaxies, and guided providentially the multibillion-year Universe-and-Earth adventure. A teenage girl, fully human and fallible, shared in the miracle of new life. The tale of Jesus' birth is not about obstetrics but Divine Presence in the chaotic wonder of this ambiguous, beautiful, fragile, and troubled world.

Mary knew the darkness of life. She experienced the anxiety of living under constant threat. At any moment and without explanation, an occupying Roman soldier could demand her obedience, even her virginity. She never experienced a moment of the freedom that we take for granted today, and yet she said "yes" to a greater Sovereignty than Caesar or Herod.

Meanwhile, her fiancé Joseph was overwhelmed with ambiguity. No doubt, he was initially skeptical of Mary's explanation; Divine conceptions are unheard of, especially among working-class girls. But finally, he too accepted the impossible. He believed the angelic visitor and came to trust the fidelity of Mary and the unexpected presence of the Divine in human flesh.

The angel says "fear not" to Mary and Joseph—and angels continue to say "fear not" to us. We are often afraid as we ponder the fate of the Earth, observe the machinations of thoughtless and heartless political leaders, face our own inner demons, and worry about the world our children and grandchildren will inherit. And yet God's call is to believe the impossible, to let go of our fears, and give birth to the Christ Child in our time.

As I write these words, I am pondering the yearly Christmas pageant at our church. In the pageant, we re-create something incredible. As we take our place at the stable, a handful of angels, shepherds, Magi, and even a bear and shark, we become contemporaries of Mary, Joseph, the Magi, and the shepherds. Christ's birth comes to us in an historic Congregational church, not unlike the one Madeleine L'Engle attended in Goshen, Connecticut. We hear the angelic message and in spite of our fears, our hearts are filled with joy. There is a chance that we will say "yes" to the impossible in our time—"Peace on earth, goodwill to all."

A CHRISTMAS PRACTICE

Today, pay attention to angelic appearances in the course of your daily activities. Scripture says that we need to practice hospitality and awareness, for we might be entertaining angels unawares. Listen for angels coming in the form of synchronous encounters, phone calls and e-mails, hunches and intuitions, dreams, and inspiration. Listen to your life, and the life that is all around you. As you consider angels in your life, take a moment to ponder what "impossible" thing God is asking you to embrace today. "Impossibilities" are not necessarily big things; they are simply big for you at this moment in time—such as letting go of a nonproductive habit, reaching out to a stranger,

I WONDER AS I WANDER

going out of your comfort zone on a political or social issue, or saying "yes" to a possibility that has been on the horizon but you've put off for far too long. Prayerfully go through your day. Stop to notice God's presence and say "yes" to God's calls in the moments of everyday life.

A CHRISTMAS PRAYER

"O come, O come, Emmanuel!"
Let your wisdom and love dwell in me.
Let me be awake and open
to angelic visitations
and impossible possibilities.
Let me open to God's Child
being born in my life,
and help me be a midwife to Christ's birth
in those around me.
In Christ's Name,
Amen.

.6.

THE FIRST DAY OF CHRISTMAS

DECEMBER 25

In those days a decree went out from Emperor Augustus that all the world should be registered. This was the first registration and was taken

while Quirinius was governor of Syria. All went to their own towns to be registered. Joseph also went from the town of Nazareth in Galilee to Judea, to the city of David called Bethlehem, because he was descended from the house and family of David. He went to be registered with Mary, to whom he was engaged and who was expecting a child. While they were there, the time came for her to deliver her child. And she gave birth to her firstborn son and wrapped him in bands of cloth, and laid him in a manger, because there was no place for them in the inn.

(Luke 2:1–7)

The neutrino and unicorn danced the
night Christ was born.

(Madeleine L'Engle, *The Genesis Trilogy*)

This Christmas evoked
in me that response
which makes me
continue to understand,
with the mind and the heart,
the love of God for his creation,
a love which is expressed
in the Incarnation.

> That tiny helpless baby
> whose birth we honor
> contained the power
> behind the universe,
> helpless, at the mercy
> of its own creation.

(Madeleine L'Engle, *The Irrational Season*)

I love Hallmark movies and the magic of Christmas they portray with snow, joyful celebrations, and the kiss under the mistletoe that portends "happily ever after" for the lucky couple. But the first Christmas was anything but romantic and blissful.

Yes, Mary and Joseph knew that their child was special. They may still have been basking in the afterglow of angelic visitations. Still, the birth of Jesus mirrors the harsh realities countless families face today—a family stranded in an unfamiliar town, with no place to stay, few resources, and little comfort or companionship on the most important day of their married life, the birth of their first child. Like millions of families today, Mary and Joseph lived in tyranny. They had no political freedom and no doubt experienced daily indignities, not to mention arbitrary threats from the occupying forces. "Taxation without representation" was no tea-party slogan for them; it was the day-to-day reality that brought them to Bethlehem that first Christmas. And soon after Christ's birth, according to Luke's Gospel, the Holy Family fled to Egypt, like the political refugees who flood from Syria to Europe and cross the border from Mexico into the United States. Christmas is no abstraction; it is the concrete story of a couple, struggling to find a home for their firstborn.

This year, I had a Mary-and-Joseph moment, except that it was Joseph and Deidre who came to my study, having just been kicked out of their home. They were pregnant, unemployed, and estranged from their families. They also had a history that put them on the wrong side of the tracks in terms of habit and lifestyle. Recovery from addiction and the reality of poverty characterized their current situation. Like thousands in North America today, they were simply looking for a room at the inn and acceptance from a stranger.

Each day, over 350,000 babies are born on Planet Earth, and the majority come into families much like Joseph and Deidre's, without any of the benefits of privilege that include a nice home, health care, working parents, an intact family, health insurance, and a healthy environment and school systems to nurture their young minds. A large portion of these babies are born into poverty and political uncertainty. Jesus was born in an occupied land, and so are the babies born this Christmas in Jesus' birthplace, Bethlehem in Palestine.

If the Incarnation means anything at all, it means that the Love of God takes birth in the complexities of our lives and that Christ is born in every child, and every family is a Holy Family. The Incarnation is more than a metaphysical abstraction—the presence of the Infinite in the finite and the Eternal in the temporary; it is the Incarnation made flesh in the real flesh-and-bone experiences of violence, insecurity, and marginalization. God experiences the pain—and joy— of the world right along with us.

Emmanuel, "God with us," is right here under my Christmas tree, well-stocked with presents, as I await a Christmas morning breakfast of quiche and coffee cake and enjoy a hot cup of coffee laced with Bailey's. God is also with us in the family mourning a child, the victim of senseless violence and our addiction to gun ownership; the Syrian refugee family eking a living in a camp in Greece; a recently married young man whose appetite has been sapped by chemotherapy treatments; a child, neglected by his high-society parents who give her everything but love; and in Joseph and Deidre and thousands of young families simply looking for a job and a place to stay. God is the fellow sufferer who understands, and the fellow celebrant who rejoices. Only a suffering God, who shares our joys and sorrows, can bring salvation to us and our world.

The world is filled with pain, and there are more than enough tears to fill the seven seas. Jesus lived through our pain and suffering—but there is also great joy, because God has come, and in God's coming we find hope for the struggle, strength for the journey, and companionship on the road that lies ahead.

Joy to the world, this wonderful and tragic world—the Lord is come!

A CHRISTMAS PRACTICE

Therese of Lisieux counseled her companions in the monastery to do ordinary things with great love. Without love, all our spiritual practices are in vain; in the words of 1 Corinthians 13, without love, we are like noisy gongs or clanging cymbals, ultimately gaining nothing from our efforts.

Let love be your goal today, whether in your interactions with family, friends, and co-workers or in your willingness to reach out in tangible ways to the vulnerable and forgotten members of your community. Prayerfully make a casserole for the local shelter or soup kitchen, and as you cook, visualize lovingly those who will benefit from your cuisine. Make an appointment to serve breakfast to the homeless—or tutor a child when school begins again in January. Prayerfully call your representatives to advocate for vulnerable, unemployed, and homeless persons and hospitality to political refugees.

A CHRISTMAS PRAYER

"Be near me, Lord Jesus,
I ask you to stay close by me forever,
and love me, I pray.
Bless all the dear children in your tender care,
and fit us for heaven, to live with you there."
On this winter eve, bless everyone
who is experiencing homelessness
and unemployment.
Bless everyone who is struggling
to make ends meet.
Bless the undocumented worker
and the citizen who is worried that
immigrants will take his job.
And let me be a channel of blessing,
bringing joy to every task and care
and to everyone I meet.
In Jesus' Name,
Amen.

.7.

THE SECOND DAY
OF CHRISTMAS

DECEMBER 26

THE FEAST OF ST. STEPHEN

In that region there were shepherds living in the fields, keeping watch over their flock by night. Then an angel of the Lord stood before them, and the glory of the Lord shone around them, and they were terrified. But the angel said to them, "Do not be afraid; for see—I am bringing you good news of great joy for all the people: to you is born this day in the city of David a Savior, who is the Messiah, the Lord. This will be a sign for you: you will find a child wrapped in bands of cloth and lying in a manger." And suddenly there was with the angel a multitude of the heavenly host, praising God and saying, "Glory to God in the highest heaven, and on earth peace among those whom he favors!"

When the angels had left them and gone into heaven, the shepherds said to one another, "Let us go now to Bethlehem and see this thing that has taken place, which the Lord has made known to us." So they went with haste and found Mary and Joseph, and the child lying in the manger. When they saw this, they made known what had been told them about this child; and all who heard it were amazed at what the shepherds told them.

But Mary treasured all these words and pondered them in her heart. The shepherds returned, glorifying and praising God for all they had heard and seen, as it had been told them.

(Luke 2:8–20)

God sends angels in unexpected
and mysterious ways . . .
we are asked to be angels–
messengers of healing and love–
whether we are aware of it or not.
We are called to be angels
not by the God Out There,
but the God In Here, with us, Emmanuel.
May God continue to send angels.
May we continue to hear.

(Madeleine L'Engle, *The Genesis Trilogy*)

In this year's Christmas pageant, one of my grandsons was a shepherd, the other a lamb. In the warmth of our simple Congregationalist sanctuary, we remembered the story of

Jesus' birth and the wonder of God's presence in a Bethlehem stable. And Grandpa, "Pastor Bruce," was an unexpected angel, Gabriel, filling an angelic void and doing double duty as a star-carrier!

God appears in unexpected places and to unlikely people. Imagine the amazement, not to mention terror, of the shepherds when the angel of God came to them with an announcement of the Divine Child's birth. The angelic visitation is both spiritual and political—and the two can't be separated—for in the Christmas stories, God comes to the forgotten, working class, the marginalized, not the affluent, powerful, and privileged. God calls these humble shepherds to move from being marginalized to becoming messengers of grace and transformation. The Divine One challenges the weak and powerless to do great things. God also challenges the downtrodden to see themselves as worthy of God's love and claim their dignity as God's children.

Two years ago, on Boxing Day (December 26), my wife and I picked out a little ball of fur to be our newest family member. This Christmas, Tucker, a golden doodle, is over eighty pounds and careens around our house full of life and love. From something small, great things emerge. From the unpromising outsiders, like the shepherds or young Madeleine L'Engle whose teachers often doubted her intellectual ability, wondrous voices of God arise.

December 26 is also celebrated as the Day of St. Stephen the Martyr, described in the words of Acts 7. Inspired by his Pentecost experience, Stephen proclaimed the good news of the risen Jesus, despite the threats of the religious and political leaders who eventually arrested and convicted him of a capital crime. As he lay dying, Stephen saw the heavens open up and was inspired to speak forgiveness to those who were killing him, including young Saul who later become Paul the Apostle. Stephen affirmed that God's revelation reaches far beyond the temples and churches to reach all Creation.

Let us in the spirit of the shepherds and the saint awaken to angelic visitations among forgotten and vulnerable persons. Let us give birth to angels in our own lives as God's messengers in our own chaotic and fragile world!

A CHRISTMAS PRACTICE

Today, ask God to send angels of wisdom and inspiration into your life. Open yourself to your own angelic vocation as a messenger of healing and love. Look throughout today for angelic moments, where you may have the opportunity to bring light to the darkness of our world. Keep your eyes open to God-sightings throughout the day and take your place as a messenger of grace if the occasion arises.

A CHRISTMAS PRAYER

Like Good King Wenceslas on the Feast of Stephen,
let us look out from our warm dwellings
at those who are poor and forgotten among us.
Let us bring "alms," not as superiors
but as brothers and sisters,
joined in an intricate fabric of relatedness.
Let us receive others' gifts as we give our own.
In Christ's Name,
Amen.

8

THE THIRD DAY OF CHRISTMAS

DECEMBER 27

In the beginning was the Word, and the Word was with God, and the Word was God. He was in the beginning with God. All things came into being through him, and without him not one thing came into being. What has come into being in him was life, and the life was the light of all people. The light shines in the darkness, and the darkness did not overcome it....

The true light, which enlightens everyone, was coming into the world.

(John 1:1–5, 9)

Cribbed, cabined, and confined
within the contours of a human infant.
The infinite defined by the finite?
The creator of life
thirsty and abandoned?
Why would he do such a thing?
Aren't there easier and better ways
for God to redeem his creatures?

(Madeleine L'Engle, *The Irrational Season*)

Christmas tells the amazing story of God's Word and Wisdom, the creative power of the universe, made flesh in finite
and fallible humankind. Beware, Christian exclusivists; God's
revelation is larger than any religious system, including Christianity. God has many faces and revelations. Wherever there
is truth and healing, God is its source, even if the name of
Jesus is never mentioned.

Despite the anxious possessiveness of those who limit revelation and salvation to Christian orthodoxy, Christian universalism is good news for all people. God's grace is unlimited, and God's quest to save us can never be defeated by the forces of evil and human sinfulness. The tyrants and demagogues of the world come and go, but God's love endures forever. Jesus is still loved and followed, while Nero, Domitian, and Hitler are consigned to the ash heaps of history.

God's true Light enlightens everyone. Buddhists, Hindus, Muslims, agnostics, and atheists are all embraced by God's universal love. With John the Evangelist, whose faith we celebrate today, we proclaim that God's light excludes no one and heals everyone. Wherever healing and love abound, this light still shines.

The Divine One comes to us all in a helpless infant. God's love is birthed in an occupied nation. God feels our pain and shares our growth from infancy to death. The Word and Wisdom of God, Logos and Sophia, guide and inspire us in our own quest to be companions, feeling the pain of the lost and grief of the lonely as we seek to play our role in healing the world.

A CHRISTMAS PRACTICE

Today, we are called to see the light and be the light. We begin with a moment of meditation:

Pause and relax in a comfortable position. Breathe deeply and slowly, letting the breath of God fill you from head to toe. After a few minutes, visualize light filling you fully with each breath, bringing healing and enlightenment. Visualize in the course of your meditation one (or more) persons filled and surrounded by God's light. Visualize God's light surrounding every encounter that you anticipate throughout the day. Visualize light shining in and through everyone you meet.

A CHRISTMAS PRAYER

"Silent night, holy night!
Son of God, love's pure light
radiant beams from Thy holy face
with the dawn of redeeming grace."
Jesus, let your light shine in and through me,
bringing light and healing to everyone I meet.
Let me see light and let me be light
in every situation in which I find myself.
In God's Light,
Amen.

9

THE FOURTH DAY OF CHRISTMAS

DECEMBER 28

When Herod saw that he had been
tricked by the wise men,
he was infuriated,
and he sent and killed
all the children in and
around Bethlehem

who were two years old or under,
according to the time that he had
learned from the wise men.

(Matthew 2:16–17)

The excitement of the arrival of
wealthy Gentile astrologers,
bringing worship and exotic gifts to the
feet of a Jewish baby,
resulted later in the
awful weight of pain
Mary must have felt at Herod's
massacre of infants.
She realized that her own little one
was protected at the expense
of all the baby boys of Bethlehem
who died in Jesus' place.

(Madeleine L'Engle, *Winter Song*)

In the words of Alfred North Whitehead, the Christmas story reveals the "tragic beauty" of the human adventure. Life begins with a dream, confronts harsh reality, and is fulfilled, we hope, in the integration of suffering, hope, and healing. On December 28, we remember the Holy Innocents, the young children—toddlers—massacred in Bethlehem, the victims of Herod's desperate plan to eliminate the newborn king. Surely, Mary, Joseph, and eventually Jesus, came to know the terrible cost of his birth and survival. Perhaps, this awareness inspired Jesus' particular love for children with whom he prayed and played, and recognized as equals in the realm of God.

You must be like a child to enter God's realm. Christmas brings out the child in even the most "mature" and cynical among us. Our hearts of stone are transformed into beating hearts of amazement and compassion as we hear and view the tales of Christmas—Dickens' *Christmas Carol*, or the movies *It's a Wonderful Life* and *Miracle on 34th Street*. The Christmas magic portrayed in story and film reminds us that through the movements of an often-unseen providence, we can begin again, as we experience a deeper, purer love.

And yet, we witness the "slaughter of innocents," not just in Matthew's account but in everyday life. Children are sacrificed for political gain, military victory, or to enrich the coffers of the wealthy. As much as some of us proclaim the sacredness of life, their care for innocent lives often ends at childbirth; programs for young mothers and children are slashed, support of schools and libraries decreased, and health-care benefits reduced, while tax policies favor the wealthy. The tears of the parents in Bethlehem still fall among refugees from Syria, Myanmar, and Central America, as well as North American parents unable to provide adequate diets, housing, and health care for their children. The slogan "it's a child not a choice" applies equally to the decisions of political and business leaders planning reduction in social service programs as it does to pregnant mothers considering abortion!

The child in us and the Child of Bethlehem demand that we listen to the children crying. The flight of the Holy Family inspires hospitality to strangers, whether they are undocumented or here legally. Christmas reminds us to offer life-giving options to children, and to ask ourselves first, "How may we ensure that each child has enough to flourish?" and then, "Do our national and local policies bring joy and health to children's lives?"

A CHRISTMAS PRACTICE

Today, let the child in you come forth. Do something silly, imaginative, and joyful; something that has no pragmatic value and offers no financial gain. Sing, dance, skip, or play with a child. Draw a picture or write a poem.

As you awaken to the child within, take a moment to visualize the children in your life, praying for each one. If you belong to a religious community, pray for the children of your congregation. Commit to doing something tangible to benefit children in your congregation, community, or the nation: call a local school about reading with a child or tutoring in a subject of your expertise; look at the newspaper or online, noting articles about at-risk children. Hold these situations in prayer, asking God to guide you to an appropriate action, such as calling a local or national representative regarding political policies that harm children, joining a advocacy group (for example, Grandmothers [or Mothers] Against Gun Violence) or contributing through a local charity a Christmas gift for a child in need.

A CHRISTMAS PRAYER

"O holy Child of Bethlehem

Descend to us, we pray. . . .

O come to us, abide with us

Our Lord Emmanuel."

Awaken the playful and loving child in me.

Bless all your children everywhere,

and open my heart

to their laughter and tears.

In the Name of the Holy Child,

Amen.

.10.

THE FIFTH DAY OF CHRISTMAS

DECEMBER 29

Now after they had left, an angel of the Lord appeared to Joseph in a dream and said, "Get up, take the child and his mother, and flee to Egypt, and remain there until I tell you; for Herod is about to search for the child, to destroy him." Then Joseph got up, took the child and his mother by night, and went to Egypt, and remained there until the death of Herod. This was to fulfill what had been spoken by the Lord through the prophet, "Out of Egypt I have called my son."

(Matthew 2:13–15)

"If a star's dying matters,
so does a person's."
"To you and me, but to the universe?"
"I don't think size matters. Every death
is a singularity. . . .
Think of all the tiny organisms
within us.
Somehow I think that every
mitochondrion and farandola
has to be just as important
as a giant star."

(Madeleine L'Engle, *A Ring of Endless Light*)

When the Holy Family left Bethlehem, probably nobody noticed their departure. Who notices the absence of a lower middle-class family or the fleeing of persons for political, economic, or personal safety reasons? Jesus and his family may have been one of many who sought asylum in Egypt during the time of Rome's occupation of Judea.

Refugee families also abound in our time, and we too give them little consideration or notice, except to see them as threats, nuisances, or job-takers. Yet, every child and her parent are known by God. If God is omnipresent, then everything in the universe is fully present to God. Every person and atom are at the center of God's universe, known by name and identity, and treasured as part of God's evolving adventure.

Once again, the Scriptures proclaim the power of a dream to change our lives. Long before Carl Jung's theories of dreams as messages of unconscious wisdom, the Jewish people took dreams seriously as revelations of Divine Wisdom, warning, protecting, guiding, and inspiring humankind. A dream saves the Holy Family.

But, more than a dream ensures their survival. Despite their immigrant—and dare we say, undocumented—status, they receive a welcome in Egypt. Despite the likely concerns about Jewish immigrants and their impact on Egypt's economy, the residents there must have taken Mary, Joseph, and Jesus into their homes and helped Joseph find work as an artisan. Someone saw the Holy Family for what they were, God's beloved children, just as every refugee and immigrant is also God's beloved child.

Those who follow Jesus are counterculture in spirit: they recognize that every immigrant matters, every refugee is important, and they know, in the spirit of Matthew 25, that the nations—and not just individuals—will be judged by how they respond to the least of these people. In the footsteps of Thomas Becket, whose death is remembered on December 29, the church must follow God's vision rather than the state's and challenge the state whenever it places political ideology, profit, or power about human and planetary well-being.

A CHRISTMAS PRACTICE

You can pray with your eyes open! Today, go online and look for photographs of refugee families. Find a particular family on which to focus. Visualize God's love surrounding them and pray for their safe passage and well-being.

Next, take some time online to research groups that advocate or support refugees. Some reputable groups include: Church World Service, US Conference of Catholic Bishops, International Rescue Committee, UNICEF, and World Vision. If you are able, make a financial contribution to a group whose work and beliefs inspire you.

A CHRISTMAS PRAYER

We hear the carol,

"Children, go where I send thee,"

and ask, "How will you send me?"

Help me to nurture the child within,

and reach out to all the children

in "your tender care."

Help me to speak on behalf of refugee children

and their parents as I work

"for peace on earth, goodwill to all."

In the Name of our Refugee Savior,

Amen.

11

THE SIXTH DAY OF CHRISTMAS

DECEMBER 30

Praise the LORD!
Praise the LORD from the heavens;
praise him in the heights!
Praise him, all his angels;
praise him, all his host!
Praise him, sun and moon;

praise him, all you shining stars!
Praise him, you highest heavens,
and you waters above the heavens!
you sea monsters and all deeps,
fire and hail, snow and frost,
stormy wind fulfilling his command!
Mountains and all hills,
fruit trees and all cedars!
Wild animals and all cattle,
creeping things and flying birds!
Kings of the earth and all peoples,
princes and all rulers of the earth!
Young men and women alike,
old and young together!

(Psalm 148:1–4, 7–12)

A whole series of pictures
came flashing across my eyes,
in the dream part of my head.
The ocean.
Rain.
A rainbow, glittering with rain.

Snow, falling in great white blossoms
to disappear as it touched the sea.
And, then the snow turned into stars,
stars in the daytime,
drenched in sunlight,
becoming sunlight, and the sunlight
was the swirling movement of a galaxy
and the ocean caught the light and was
part of the galaxy
and the stars of the galaxies
lifted butterfly wings
and flew together dancing.

(Madeleine L'Engle, *A Ring of Endless Light*)

The Christmas spirit inspires the mystic in all of us. The Spirit of God shines in a stable in Bethlehem and bursts forth in our cells as well as our souls. The morning stars sing God's praises and a star in the East guides Magi to a Child who is God Incarnate. This is the mystical vision revealed in *A Wind in the Door*, where Madeleine L'Engle describes farandolae, microscopic energy units that energize subcellular mitochondria, dancing in harmony with Divine Wisdom. The micro and macro reveal God's wisdom, and both are essential to our personal and planetary well-being.

In the spirit of Celtic spirituality, the Christmas message is that thin places, translucent to God, are everywhere. Goodness is everywhere. It abounds in the most unexpected places.

Keeping the spirit of Christmas throughout the year involves paying attention to the world around us and within us, and pausing long enough to notice and give thanks for the wonders of Creation. The only appropriate response to the Incarnation is radical amazement and awareness that the heavens declare the glory of God, the birds of the air sing God's praises, and a little Child, the baby of Bethlehem—and the children in our own lives—have given birth to God in ordinary time. Inspired by the Incarnation, we become Christ-bearers ourselves, bringing hope and healing to every task. Like Frances Joseph-Gaudet, a prison reformer of mixed-race heritage, honored as a saint by the Episcopal Church on December 30, we can experience and then bring forth the light of God in the most hopeless situations, among prisoners, persons experiencing homelessness, and refugees.

A CHRISTMAS PRACTICE

Once again, pray with your eyes open. Pause often throughout the day to experience the beauty of the world. Let your senses be bathed in wonder as you gaze at the stars above and at your own face in the mirror. Be amazed at falling snow, gentle breezes, and chirping birds, all declaring God's glory. Give thanks throughout the day for the beauty of the Earth and the universe around us.

A CHRISTMAS PRAYER

"Joy to the world,"
the Child is come to us in Bethlehem,
in birdsong and flying geese,
in right whales and plankton,
in flowing waters and long, dark nights.
Help me to celebrate

the "wonders of your love," O Creator,

each moment and every day.

In Christ's Name,

Amen.

12

THE SEVENTH DAY OF CHRISTMAS

DECEMBER 31

I am about to do a new thing;
now it springs forth,
do you not perceive it?

I will make a way in the wilderness
and rivers in the desert.

(Isaiah 43:19)

Look God,
you took big handfuls of chaos
and made galaxies
and stars and solar systems
and night and day and sun and rain
and snow and me.
I take paint and crayon and paper
and make worlds, too,
along with you.

(Madeleine L'Engle, *Winter Song*)

On New Year's Eve, we hope for a new thing. The past is too much with us, and we are tired of it. We have seen the foolishness and greed of national leaders, the rise of white supremacist groups, the war on the poor for the sake of personal profit and corporate gain, and the disregard of our impact on the Earth by those in power. We have been overwhelmed by the culture of death, perpetuated by the leaders of nations, business, and even religious institutions.

God's word to the prophet Isaiah was amazing nearly three thousand years ago, and it is amazing to us today. We need to remember that the moral arc bends toward justice, despite the apparent victory of the powers of evil. The light shines in the darkness and the darkness cannot overcome it.

Jewish mystics say that the world is saved one person at a time. I believe that the process of *tikkun olam* (repairing the world) also occurs one moment, one action, one thought at a time. We are called to be companions in co-creation, partners with God in bringing the world of Shalom to birth in our world. It's up to us to turn the song of creation toward life rather than death, influencing cells, souls, and solar systems. We can't wait for others to change the world. We are the ones we've been waiting for, as poet June Jordan says in her "Poem for South African Women." We must become the change we want to see in the world, as Mahatma Gandhi counseled and President Barack Obama popularized.

God spins the solar systems, and my grandchildren create worlds, too, with their drawing and storytelling. All of us can be God's companions in world-shaping. We can change the climate of our communities, nation, and planet. With John Wycliffe (1320–1385), celebrated this day by the Church of England, we can share in God's work by making God's good news—as Wycliffe did with the Bible—available to all people. In the darkest night when our nation has lost its spiritual GPS, we need to pay attention to God's new thing being birthed and claim our role as midwives of Divine healing in our time.

A CHRISTMAS PRACTICE

You are a mystic and you are an artist. Let the artist in you emerge today. Prayerfully write a poem, draw a picture, recall a story from your childhood (perhaps a Christmas past) and commit it to paper, sing a song, or play an instrument, all to the glory of God. Feel free to share your stories with a special friend or family member.

A CHRISTMAS PRAYER

Awaken me to the music of the spheres
and the glories of Creation.
Help me to "dance at a new baby's birth"
and "make music in an old person's heart."
Let me be an artist of creation,
co-creating a beautiful world with you,
O Divine Artist,
Amen

.13.

THE EIGHTH DAY OF CHRISTMAS

JANUARY 1

After eight days had passed, it was time to circumcise the child; and he was called Jesus, the name given by the angel before he was conceived in the womb. When the time came for their purification according to the law of Moses, they brought him up to Jerusalem to

present him to the Lord (as it is written in the law of the Lord, "Every first-born male shall be designated as holy to the Lord"), and they offered a sacrifice according to what is stated in the law of the Lord, "a pair of turtledoves or two young pigeons."

(Luke 2:21–24)

What is the nature of time?
of creation? of life?
What is human creativity?
What is our share in God's work?...
Unless we are creators
we are not fully alive.

(Madeleine L'Engle, *Walking on Water*)

Words matter. Names matter.

In the Jewish tradition, boys are given names on the eighth day, the day of their circumcision. And so it was that two millennia ago, on the eighth day after their baby boy's birth, a lower middle-class family came unnoticed to the

Temple with a modest gift. They named their son "Yeshua," or "Jesus," which means "Yahweh is our salvation." No one noticed Jesus and his family, except two elders.

To the ancients, names meant something—and they still mean something today. African American mystic Howard Thurman describes the impact of Morehouse University's President John Hope's words on marginalized and down-trodden African American young men, during a time in which their fathers were often addressed as "boy":

He always addressed us as "young gentlemen." What this term of respect meant to our faltering egos can only be understood against the backdrop of the South of the 1920s. We were black men in Atlanta during a period in which Georgia was infamous for its racial brutality. Lynchings, burnings, unspeakable cruelties were the fundamentals of existence for black people. Our physical lives were of little value. Any encounter with a white person was inherently dangerous and frequently fatal. Those of us who managed to remain physically whole found our lives defined in less than human terms.

What names do you give the ones around you—your life partner, children, friends, strangers, people of other faiths or ethnicities? Many citizens think of "terrorist," when they hear the word "Islam" or "Muslim." An American political leader referred to Mexican immigrants as "murderers" and "rapists," despite the fact that most Muslims are good, law-abiding, productive citizens; and most Mexican immigrants, whether documented or undocumented, go to work, raise families, pay taxes, are necessary to the American economy, and hope for a better life for their children.

Words matter. Names matter. I strive to use affirmative language to describe my companions and family, based on my belief that we are all God's beloved children, worthy of love, and possessing that indefinable yet life-transforming image of God. As Madeleine L'Engle asserts: "Every star in the sky is unique, every leaf on a tree, every snowflake, every farandola, every cherubim, unique: Named" (*A Wind at the Door*).

What is your true name? Do you know? In the Christmas season, Jesus is named "God is our salvation"—and in that name, we discover both the infinite depth of God's love for us and our own identities that arise out of our vocation to love one another.

A CHRISTMAS PRACTICE

Many people have found the use of spiritual affirmations life-transforming. Their use of affirmations begins as a mental practice, and then slowly begins to shape conscious and unconscious attitudes, self-image, perception, and behavior.

Take time now to reflect on your internal dialogue: what words or images characterize your self-understanding? What words emerge when you think about other people, including marginalized persons? Do you criticize or affirm those around you? Do you tend to praise or blame?

In the Christmas season, you might use affirmations such as the following:

- I am following God's star throughout the day.
- God's word is made flesh in my daily life and actions.
- I awaken to angelic encounters.

- God is giving me healing and enlightening dreams.
- God's light brings healing to my body, mind, and spirit.

Repeat these or other affirmations throughout the day. Let them become the lens through which you view your life, daily encounters, and social involvement.

A CHRISTMAS PRAYER

Holy One, whose Child
is our "childhood's pattern," help us
to grow like the One who came to save us.
Teach us to see God's emerging growth
and potential in ourselves
and in everyone we meet.
May we find our true-nature Names
as your beloved children.
In the Name of the One who Names us,
Amen.

.14.

THE NINTH DAY
OF CHRISTMAS

JANUARY 2

Now there was a man in Jerusalem whose name was Simeon; this man was righteous and devout, looking forward to the consolation of Israel, and the Holy Spirit rested on him. It had been revealed to him by the Holy Spirit that he would not see death before he had seen the Lord's Messiah. Guided by the Spirit, Simeon came into the temple; and when the parents brought in the child Jesus, to do for him what was customary under the law, Simeon took him in his arms and praised God, saying,"Master, now you are dismissing your servant in peace, according to your word; for my eyes have seen your salvation, which you have prepared in the presence of all peoples, a light for revelation to the Gentiles and for glory to your people Israel."

And the child's father and mother were amazed at what was being said about him. Then Simeon blessed them and said to his mother Mary, "This child is destined for the falling and the rising of many in Israel, and to be a sign that will be opposed so that the inner thoughts of many will be revealed—and a sword will pierce your own soul too."

There was also a prophet, Anna the daughter of Phanuel, of the tribe of Asher. She was of a great age, having lived with her husband seven years after her marriage, then as a widow to the age

I WONDER AS I WANDER

of eighty-four. She never left the temple but worshiped there with fasting and prayer night and day. At that moment she came, and began to praise God and to speak about the child to all who were looking for the redemption of Jerusalem.

(Luke 2:25–38)

When Mother closed the book, we turned out the lights and said prayers. We have a couple of family prayers and Our Father and we say to each other God Bless. Rob is very personal about his God Bless. He puts in anything that he feels like. . . . Last Christmas, for instance, in the middle of his God Bless, he said "Oh, God bless Santa Claus and bless you, too, God."

(Madeleine L'Engle, *The Irrational Season*)

"And, bless you, too, God."

Does God need our blessings? Does God need words and thoughts that nurture God's happiness and well-being?

I believe God does. In an interdependent universe, knitted together in an intricate fabric of relatedness, when we bless one another, we also bless God. When we give to the "least of these," we also enrich God's experience.

Therese of Lisieux counseled, "Do ordinary things with love." Her namesake Saint Teresa of Calcutta invited us to "do something beautiful for God." Loving God and loving Creation reflect an appreciation and affirmation of life. When we love God rightly, we wisely respond to the needs of Creation. Loving God leads to reverence for life and positive actions to bring beauty to the world. When we rightly love creatures, our love flows from earth to heaven, bringing joy to God's experience of the world.

January 2 celebrates the fourth-century theologian, Gregory of Nazianzus, known most for his role in articulating the doctrine of the Trinity. Although the Trinity—the dynamic and intricate unity of the three persons of the Godhead—will always be a mystery that defies "orthodox" attempts at strict definition, the Threeness of God points to the integrity of God's relationship with the world. There is no "bait and switch" in God's grace. Jesus of Nazareth reflects God's graceful will and love for Creation, and the Spirit brings joy to the world. Although we can never fully fathom God, there is no "hidden" God, whose purposes contradict the hospitality, healing, and sacrificial love present in Jesus of Nazareth, the Christ. Moreover, the Trinity also reflects God's own inner and outer complexity and diversity. God is alive, dynamic, and multifaceted in God's nature and relationship with the world.

The world God creates is also lively, dynamic, and diverse. Diversity is a blessing that reflects God's nature, whether in the diverse cultures, ethnicities, and religions of humankind, or our understandings of God. God does not want uniformity in worship, spiritual practice, or institutional structures; God delights in multiplicity. Every authentic spiritual path is blessed by God and should be blessed by us.

As we take our first steps into the new year, what beauty can we add to the world one moment at a time? What beauty can we give to God in our daily lives?

A CHRISTMAS PRACTICE

Today, once again, pray with your eyes open, giving thanks for the diversity of the world—the diverse cultures and religions, the diverse colors of trees, plants, and homes, the diverse colors and lifestyles of your fellow humans, the amazing diversity of flora and fauna you encounter each day. Take time to honor diversity in your words and actions.

A CHRISTMAS PRAYER

"Gloria! Gloria!"
I give you thanks for "dappled things,"
for the colors of the rainbow,
for religious and cultural diversity
and for the wonders of God's world
presented to me every waking moment.
Let me embrace and support healthy diversity,
welcoming and affirming humanity
in all its wondrous variety.
In Christ's Name,
Amen.

.15.

THE TENTH DAY OF CHRISTMAS

JANUARY 3

When they had finished everything required by the law of the Lord, they returned to Galilee, to their own town of Nazareth. The child grew and became  strong, filled with wisdom; and the favor of God was upon him.

(Luke 2:39–40)

This is our calling, co-creation.
Every single one of us,

without exception,
is called to co-create with God.
No one is too unimportant
to have a share
in the making or unmaking
of the final shining-forth.
Everything that we do either draws the
Kingdom of love closer,
or pushes it further off.

(Madeleine L'Engle, *Genesis Trilogy*)

After his naming and circumcision, Jesus' family returns home. Home is, ideally, the place of emotional, physical, and spiritual nurture, and in his home, Jesus grew to be the child God had imagined as a result of his parents' love and his own choices. God's light grew strong and loving in him.

A dozen years later, after a lively conversation with the Temple priests, Luke reports that Jesus grew in "wisdom and stature and divine and human favor" (Luke 2:52). An alternative version says, "Jesus increased in wisdom and in years," but this translation misses the richness of the word "stature." One can grow older and not necessarily wiser (as we see in the antics and bloviations of septuagenarian politicians). "Stature" suggests a largeness of spirit, an ability to entertain contrasting viewpoints without polarization or denial, an embrace of otherness, even opposition, without succumbing to bullying or exclusion.

Wisdom and stature are best learned through the interplay of home, school, and church (or other healthy religious communities). Such growth requires loving and nurturing environments and a culture that encourages healthy and large-spirited families. We are the children of our environment, both near and far, as well as our day-to-day decisions.

The Christmas season reminds us to create healthy environments—economically, educationally, socially, spiritually—that enable children to reach their fullest human potential. African American mystic Howard Thurman once asserted that one of the greatest tragedies of poverty and racism was the destruction of the imagination and the diminishment of dreams, among those at the bottom end of the social order. A healthy and imaginative society requires that we nurture dreams—and dreamers—of all kinds, both citizens and the children of undocumented workers. The early Christian theologian Irenaeus once stated that the glory of

God is a fully alive human, and this should be the goal of our institutions as well as our personal journeys.

On this day, the Episcopal church remembers William Passavant, a Lutheran minister, who helped establish the deaconess movement in the United States to promote human well-being, honor women's gifts, and add to God's glory by companioning with God in healing the sick.

Some thirty years after Jesus' naming, Jesus came to Jordan to be baptized and as he came out of the water, he heard God's voice proclaiming, "You are my son, the Beloved; with you I am well pleased" (Luke 3:22). I believe God speaks these words to every child. God also speaks these words to you and invites you to make the experience of Divine Love the birthright of every child through just and compassionate social, governmental, and religious structures.

A CHRISTMAS PRACTICE

Today, we return to the use of Christmas affirmations. Throughout the day, make the following affirmations several times, especially when you are tempted to lose your spiritual focus:

- I am God's beloved son [or daughter].
- I am growing in wisdom and stature.
- I experience God's light in every encounter.

A CHRISTMAS PRAYER

Holy God,
help us to "dream of the joyous day to come"—
this day of beauty and wonder.
Let me grow as I dream,
awakening to blessings without number
and life in all its abundance.
In the Dreamer's Name,
Amen.

THE ELEVENTH DAY OF CHRISTMAS

JANUARY 4

The LORD created me at the
beginning of his work,
the first of his acts of long ago.
Ages ago I was set up, at the first,
before the beginning of the earth.

When there were no depths
I was brought forth,
when there were no springs
abounding with water.
Before the mountains had been shaped,
before the hills, I was brought forth—
when he had not yet made
earth and fields,
or the world's first bits of soil.
When he established the heavens,
I was there,
when he drew a circle
on the face of the deep,
when he made firm the skies above,
when he established
the fountains of the deep,
when he assigned to the sea its limit,
so that the waters might not transgress
his command,
when he marked out
the foundations of the earth,
then I was beside him,

like a master worker;
and I was daily his delight,
rejoicing before him always,
rejoicing in his inhabited world
and delighting in the human race.
And now, my children, listen to me:
happy are those who keep my ways.
Hear instruction and be wise,
and do not neglect it.

(Proverbs 8:22–33)

We lose our human calling
because we do not dare to be creators,
co-creators with God.

(Madeleine L'Engle, *Walking on Water*)

Now more than ever, with planetary survival pushed to the limits by the foolishness of humankind and its political leaders, we need to listen to Divine Wisdom. Often neglected, Wisdom or Sophia is the reality John's Gospel describes as the Word made flesh in the creation of the universe, the incarnation of the Christ, and the enlightening of humankind (John 1:1–5, 9). In Proverbs 8, Holy Wisdom, the feminine aspect of Divinity, moves through all things as God's partner, playmate, and artist of Creation. God delights in her cosmic playfulness and artistry in bringing forth an amazing universe.

Just look around you and behold wonders without limit. Look at your own life and experience how amazing it is even in its ambiguity and struggle. If we open our eyes to the "wonders of God's love," we will be filled with gratitude and radical amazement. When we listen to the ways of Wisdom, embedded in stars, cells, and spirits, we are in balance with one another and the world that supports us and depends upon our wise stewardship. Our creativity reflects Divine Creativity.

We are not alone in the universe. There is holiness in the hidden depths of things, in the subcellular mitochondria and farandolae Madeleine L'Engle describes in *A Wind at the Door*. Experience and value are present everywhere, even where we least expect it. The psalmist asserts that everything that breathes praises God (Psalm 150:6). Even the stars pray, as theologian Jay McDaniel affirms in his book *Living from the Center*. When God brought forth this glorious universe, "the morning stars sang together and the heavenly beings shouted for joy" (Job 38:7).

A metaphysics of beauty inspires an ethic of compassion and reverence for life. The God who hears the cries of the poor also experiences the pain of endangered species, such as the threat to the survival of North Atlantic's remaining four hundred or so right whales, many of whom make yearly treks to the waters off my home on Cape Cod. We need to love the baby humans, but we also need to love the baby right whales—and my grandchildren's favorite, pangolins, one of the world's most trafficked animal due to the delicacy of its meat and the purported healing powers of its scales.

In the spirit of Divine Wisdom, the Episcopal Church affirms on this date the work of Roman Catholic Elizabeth Ann Seton, who founded the Sisters of Charity to provide education for girls. Her work uplifted impoverished and dispossessed young girls.

The Divine Wisdom from whom all blessings flow inspires compassion, creativity, and joy in human life and in the affairs of institutions and nations. God delights in us just as God delights in Holy Wisdom (Sophia). We are invited to claim our role as creative partners in healing the Earth.

A CHRISTMAS PRACTICE

Ask God to give you a creative vision for the day ahead. Look for moments in the day when you can add to the beauty of the Earth and bring joy to those around you. If you feel passive or helpless in relationship to governmental and institutional power, ask God to give you insight in terms of how to respond to the powers and principalities, steering them toward life and creation, not death and destruction. Do one act of creative compassion in the course of the day.

A CHRISTMAS PRAYER

God of Wisdom and Light,

who brings light and life to all,

raising our spirits with "healing in his wings,"

awaken us to your wisdom.

Inspire us with your love

and guide us with your wisdom,

that we may create wisely with you

for your glory and for the healing

of our planet and our fellow creatures,

human and nonhuman alike.

In the Name of Sophia, Holy Wisdom,

Amen.

THE TWELFTH DAY OF CHRISTMAS

JANUARY 5

He is the image of the invisible God, the first-born of all creation; for in him all things in heaven and on earth were created, things visible and invisible, whether thrones or dominions or rulers or powers—all things have been created through him and for him. He himself is before all things, and in him all things hold together. He is the head of the body, the church; he is the beginning, the firstborn from the dead, so that he might come to have first place in everything. For in him all the fullness of God was pleased to dwell, and through him God was pleased to reconcile to himself all things, whether on earth or in heaven, by making peace through the blood of his cross.

(Colossians 1:15–20)

We are part of a vast web of relationships and interrelationships which sing themselves in ancient harmonies. . . . I have used the word kything, found in the old Scottish dictionary of my grandfather's, to express this communication without words, where there is "neither speech nor language." To kythe is to open yourself to someone.

(Madeleine L'Engle, *Genesis Trilogy*)

This Christmas, my two young grandsons sang a humorous variation of "The First Noel." Recently acquainted with the word "hell," they marched around the house singing "No-hell! No-hell! No-hell!" While I am not sure that they were aware of the theological ramifications of their chanting, their words pointed to an inclusive salvation—a generous, interdependent universe in which the salvation of one is connected to the salvation of all, and the salvation of the whole is dependent on the well-being of each part. If God is to be "all in all," then all Creation must eventually be redeemed and transformed into God's unique likeness for each creature.

We are part of a profoundly interdependent and intricate fabric of relatedness. In the words of Martin Luther King Jr., "We are caught in an inescapable network of mutuality; tied in a single garment of destiny. Whatever affects one directly, affects all indirectly." Theologians have described this reality in terms of the body of Christ, or beloved community, where the well-being of each and the well-being of all rise or fall together. Along the same lines, physicists and medical researchers speak of nonlocal causation or spooky action at a distance. Meteorologists describe the butterfly effect in which a butterfly flapping its wings in Pacific Grove, California, might shape weather patterns on Craigville Beach on Cape Cod, where I walk most mornings. And Madeleine L'Engle describes the profound, nonlocal interdependence of life in terms of "kything," a process by which we can feel the feelings and experience the thoughts of others across time and space.

Another word for the reality described by "kything" is prayer. Prayer connects us with others without regard to time or place. When we pray, our thoughts and feelings become part of the reality others experience at an unconscious level. In prayer, we enhance God's energy of love. We enable God's vision of wholeness to be embodied more fully in the lives of others and in the world at large.

Medical researchers have pondered the power of prayer, and studies suggest that persons who are prayed for may have better health outcomes than those who are not. Although I believe prayer changes things, I have trouble taking these studies literally insofar as I am uncertain if we can find a "control" group of persons who are not the recipients of the goodwill of others. With the poet Mary Oliver, I confess that "I don't know exactly what a prayer is" ("The Summer Day"). But there are rare moments when the poet and I remember "how to pay attention" to the experiences of others, whether it be Oliver's grasshopper, my two grandchildren playing beside me as I write these words, the world's leaders, or a beloved friend.

The times call for prayer—big-spirited, hospitable, generous, and loving prayer—for us, our communities, and the good Earth. Let us "kythe" with the planet and those whom we love. Let us awaken to our calling to pray for God's new creation emerging in our world.

A CHRISTMAS PRACTICE

Today, I invite you to take an adventure in prayerfulness or kything. Let your prayers involve words, but also images and visualizations. Experience yourself connected with those for whom you pray. With Madeleine L'Engle, you may choose to visualize those for whom you pray, as well as the entire planet, as healthy and whole and aligned with God's vision of Shalom.

Prayer is a journey without distance, a nonlocal phenomenon, that connects us with a child or life partner sitting beside you, a political leader in need of wisdom, a friend across the globe, or a family member on holiday faraway. In the spirit of Celtic Christianity, prayer creates "thin places" that may even join the "living" and the "dead" in holy harmony.

A CHRISTMAS PRAYER

"Joy to the world the Lord is come!"

God is here in this holy here and now.

Join me, O God, with the beauty of Creation.

Join me in healing spirit with loved ones near and far.

Let my thoughts and feelings

bring health and wholeness to all around.

I pray this day for the full and complete healing

and restoration of [person or group].

I pray that our leaders

and in particular [name of leader]

follow the path of wisdom and peace.

I pray for endangered species and at-risk flora.

I pray to be an instrument of peace

wherever I find myself.

Let me join with the peoples of the Earth

in a hymn of unending praise.

In Christ's healing Name,

Amen.

.18.

POSTLUDE: WANDERING FORWARD

JANUARY 6

THE FEAST OF EPIPHANY

In the time of King Herod, after Jesus was born in Bethlehem of Judea, wise men from the East came to Jerusalem, asking, "Where is the child who has been born king of the Jews? For we observed his star at its rising, and have come to pay him homage." When King Herod heard this, he was frightened, and all Jerusalem with him; and calling together all the chief priests and scribes of the people, he inquired of them where the Messiah was to be born. They told him, "In Bethlehem of Judea; for so it has been written by the prophet: 'And you, Bethlehem, in the land of Judah, are by no means least among the rulers of Judah; for from you shall come a ruler who is to shepherd my people Israel.'"

Then Herod secretly called for the wise men and learned from them the exact time when the star had appeared. Then he sent them to Bethlehem, saying, "Go and search diligently for the child; and when you have found him, bring me word so that I may also go and pay him homage." When they had heard the king, they set out; and there, ahead of them, went the star that they had seen at its rising, until it stopped over the place where the child was. When they saw that the star had stopped, they were overwhelmed with joy. On entering the house, they saw the child with Mary his mother; and they knelt down and paid him homage. Then, opening their treasure chests, they offered him gifts of gold, frankincense, and myrrh. And having been warned in a dream not to return to Herod, they left for their own country by another road.

(Matthew 2:1–12)

> This is my charge to you.
> You are to be a light bearer.
> You are to choose the light.

(Madeleine L'Engle, *A Ring of Endless Light*)

On the feast of Epiphany, we remember the journey of the Magi, who prove that the breadth of Divine revelation falls beyond the boundaries of Christianity. Furthermore, God's revelation does not come to the Herods of our world—the political leaders, sure of their own personal grandeur. Instead, it comes in the form of a small child, one of the poor of the Earth, born in a barn, and soon to be a political refugee.

The first witnesses were lower-class shepherds of dubious reputation and even more dubious social standing, not worthy of consideration by the wealthy and powerful. Later witnesses were the three exotic visitors from another land and religious tradition, who had no right, according to the religious exclusivists of the time, to receive a revelation from the Holy One of Israel. Yet God's wisdom is broadcast generously across the Earth, embracing all times and places, persons of all cultures and faith traditions, the nonhuman world, and the stars and galaxies on their cosmic journeys.

An epiphany is a moment of revelation—an instantaneous new understanding of something you had never before comprehended. When we keep this definition in mind, Epiphany becomes more than a season in the Christian year. It is the ongoing manifestation of God in our world; it is the moment-by-moment experience of fresh insight into the nature of reality. Epiphanies come by grace, often unexpected and unsought for; they also emerge for those who wait, like Anna or Simeon, or those who search the heavens like the Zoroastrian Magi of the Gospels.

Epiphany is the season of wandering and wondering. As J.R.R. Tolkien noted, "not all who wander are lost." As leaders pursue with great vigor and intention the pathways of death, telling their adoring crowds how great things are despite the growing gap between the rich and poor and the continuing degradation of the Earth, we need to wander off the beaten path—and go toward our true country by another way. We need also to cultivate the spirit of wonder: to imagine impossible things, to look beyond the surface and see hidden beauty, and to discern God's face disguised by suffering, injustice, and hatred. We need to explore and not limit our exploration, looking for burning bushes around every corner and angelic faces in every encounter.

On the feast of Epiphany, we are challenged to become companions in God's never-ending adventure, guided by the horizons of wholeness and inspired by glimpses of the moral arc of history, bending toward justice and flowing through our daily lives. Let us remember the words of Mad-

eleine L'Engle as an affirmation and a prayer for the exciting
and challenging journeys that lie ahead:

> We live in an open, creative, interacting universe, and to
> try to close it in a safe little system is a danger to our-
> selves and a danger to everyone we touch. But if we are
> willing to be a small part of a great whole, then we know
> that no part of the dance is too small, too unimportant
> to make a difference. We are all like the butterfly in the
> amazing magnitude of our effect. Even when we feel
> most helpless, when events that we cannot control or
> prevent pile up, even in our most bitter brokenness, we
> do have our role in the working out of the great plan.
>
> May God, through the Christ shown to us by the
> Holy Spirit, open our hearts in love. Alleluia. (*The Genesis
> Trilogy*)

A CHRISTMAS PRACTICE

Today, commit yourself to being a light-bearer, to being a manifestation of the change you are seeking in the world, as Gandhi counseled. We cannot wait for a Divine rescue operation, or an Earth-destroying Second Coming. "We are the ones we've been waiting for," as poet June Jordan affirms. Let us make a commitment today and throughout Epiphany and in the pilgrimage ahead to bring light and love to every encounter, even when we protest injustice. May we set our minds free from walls that separate us from others, and instead may we be willing to wonder, accepting that there is much we can learn from each other and from God, and to wander, committing ourselves to adventurous exploration of new ideas and new ways of thinking. As we wander and wonder, may we truly be God's agents of healing and wholeness for our families, congregations, communities, nation, and this good Earth.

A CHRISTMAS PRAYER

"Brightest and best of the stars of the morning,

dawn on our darkness and lend us your aid,"

in this time in which leaders have

lost their moral compass

and the world is at risk.

Let your starlight and sunlight

shine in and through us,

radiating forth to bring light to the world,

love to the lonely, and hope to the fearful.

Guide my feet, so that I might

"go tell it on the mountain that

Jesus Christ is born"

right here and now in this holy moment.

Let the spirit of the Christmas star

guide me in the year ahead.

With the Magi, let my life be a gift to Jesus

and to all his children, human and nonhuman alike.

In the Name of the Way-Maker and Life-Giver,

let it be so!

I WONDER AS I WANDER

BOOKS TO LIVE BY

WANDERING WITH MADELEINE L'ENGLE

A Ring of Endless Light. New York: Bantam Doubleday Dell Books, 1980.

A Swiftly Moving Planet. New York: Farrar, Straus, and Giroux, 1978.

A Wind at the Door. New York: Farrar, Straus, and Giroux, 1973.

A Wrinkle in Time. New York: Farrar, Straus, and Giroux, 1962.

Bright Evening Star: The Mystery of the Incarnation. Colorado Springs, CO: WaterBrook Press, 1997.

The Genesis Trilogy: A Wrinkle in Time; A Wind at the Door, A Swiftly Tilting Planet. Colorado Springs, CO: WaterBrook Press, 1997.

The Irrational Season. New York: Harper and Row, 1977.

The Summer of the Great-Grandmother. New York: Farrar, Strauss, and Giroux, 1974.

Walking on Water: Reflections on Faith and Art. New York: Penguin, 2016.

Winter Song: Christmas Readings by Madeleine L'Engle and Luci Shaw. Vancouver, BC: Regent College Publishing, 1996.

THE WORK OF CHRISTMAS
The 12 Days of Christmas
with Howard Thurman

This book is a celebration of the twelve days of Christmas, offering us a chance to dwell on the meaning of the season in dialogue with the wisdom of one of America's greatest mystics and activists, Howard Thurman.

During the twelve days of Christmas, our goal is to experience God's light, despite the temptation to close our hearts in a world too often characterized by racism, sexism, polarization, nationalism, and exclusion. This season asks us instead to open our hearts and our lives, so that throughout

the year ahead, we may be light-bearers, carrying the message of Divine justice and hope, making it come alive even in the darkest corners of the world. This is the year-round work of Christmas!

Paperback Price: $10.99

Kindle Price: $5.99

BECOME FIRE!
GUIDEPOSTS FOR INTERSPIRITUAL PILGRIMS

In the spirit of God's call to creative transformation, Bruce Epperly invites you to join him on a holy adventure in spiritual growth, inspired by the evolving wisdom of Christianity and the world's great spiritual traditions, innovative global spiritual practices, and emerging visions of reality. Epperly explores the many resources of Christian spirituality in dialogue with the spiritual practices of the world's great wisdom traditions, describing the gifts other spiritual paths contribute to the pathway of Jesus; at the same time, he uses the

lens of the spiritual practices Jesus has inspired throughout Christian history to examine these spiritual paths.

Paperback Price: $24.95

Kindle Price: $8.99

SANTA CLAUS
Saint, Shaman, & Symbol

If you don't believe in Santa, you might want to reconsider. The familiar fellow dressed in red has been around a lot longer than the malls' Santa, longer than Rudolph, longer even than "The Night Before Christmas." His earliest and most ancient forms brought hope and cheer to generation after generation of humankind—and he still has a message for us today. In the midst of the materialism of the modern holiday, Santa offers us a bridge between the physical, secular world and the spiritual, sacred realm. Discover his

history and evolution, from Ice Age shaman to medieval saint to modern-day icon. Get to know Santa— and believe all over again.

Paperback Price: $12.95

Kindle Price: $5.99

BRUCE EPPERLY is pastor of South Congregational Church, Centerville, Massachusetts, and a professor in theology and spirituality at Wesley Theological Seminary, Washington, DC. He is also the author of more than forty-five books on theology, spirituality, healing, ministry, and scripture, including *The Mystic in You: Discovering a God-Filled World*, *Become Fire!: Guideposts for Interspiritual Pilgrims*, and *The Work of Christmas: The 12 Days of Christmas with Howard Thurman*. He lives on Cape Cod, where he is an avid beach walker, grandparent, husband, father, and advocate for environmental care.

ANAMCHARA
BOOKS

AnamcharaBooks.com

Made in the USA
Middletown, DE
28 December 2020

30306424R00080